Lust, Pain & Love

A Poetry Collection

DEE EVANS

Lust, Pain & Love

Copyright © 2020 Donavia (Dee) Evans

All rights reserved. No part of this publication may be reproduced, stored in a retrieval system, or transmitted in any form or by any means-for example, electronic, photocopy, recording-without the prior written permission of the publisher. The only exceptions are brief quotations in printed reviews.

All rights reserved.

For information about custom editions, special sales, premium and bulk purchases, please contact:
www.rise2write.com

Rise2Write Publishing LLC

DEDICATION

This poetry book is Dedicated to Everyone that has endured Hurt, Pain and never gave up on Love!

Lust, Pain & Love

INTRODUCTION

Poetry is formed from beautiful expressions and emotions felt within the soul. It allows you to create, explore, imagine, design, paint the picture, etc.

This grown and sexy poetry collection allows you to explore the emotions of lust, pain, and love.

Lust felt so strongly that it feels equivalent to love. Lust transitions into hurt and pain. As the reality of lust sets in, the pain develops and takes over the human emotions.

A broken spirit has overcome the thought of finding real love. Healing and acceptance allow a new path to align. An unforeseen love re-connection. A new shift of true, pure, real, genuine love.

Lust, Pain & Love

PART I

LUST

Lust, Pain & Love

SWEET LIES

Sweet lies you recite
Charming you are
My crave I hand over
Without question
Your lips
Have set the mood
Sweet Lies
Telling me all the right things
I want to feel
Yearning to hear
Setting the tone
Pacing the mood
Of the future
To come
From your sweet lips
Of Lies
Massaging my mind
Exercising my spirit
Sweet Liar

Lust, Pain & Love

CLOUD NINE

My spirit hides in the clouds
When I think of you
You take me to a euphoric place
Beyond measurable
Cloud Nine
I am On
When your body touches mine
Your lips feel like heaven
So soft so pure
Lick me slow
From head to toe
Tongue me down until my breath
Is lost in the clouds
Off your love
Your spirit and soul
I feel when I am with you
I love this feeling
Is it real
Is this permanent
Or
Am I just a Visitor?
In the clouds
On cloud nine

Lust, Pain & Love

LISTENER

Great listener
You are
Better than the rest
Effectively listening
While gazing into my heart
Caressing my ecstasy against yours
Putting me at ease
As I tell you all my dreams and goals
My desires and wants
As you cosign my value
The respect that was needed
But never granted
When I tell you
About my past and present
You could almost vomit
My heartbreaks and weakest moments
My pain and trauma
You kneeled to hold me close
Great listener
You are
Do not use it Against me!

Lust, Pain & Love

CHARMER

Charming to me
You grab my soul
So deeply
All attention
I am at ease
Can't sleep
Without you in my dreams
In my ears
Whispering to me
You will never leave
You want it badly
Charming my heart over
Misleading to believe
You have come to protect it
From the misery
Charmer get back
Before you hurt me!

Lust, Pain & Love

___SIZE___

Not big
Not small
Poppin pills
To extend the size
Thick in width
Circumcision arises
Great whale
Motion in the ocean
Shark knock off
What an illusion
All in size
Depends on the day
Of deception!

Lust, Pain & Love

BIRTHDAY SEX

Come closer
Undress your clothing
Naked soul to soul
As I reach to grab your girth
Allow me in
I want to feel that big ego
Your so blessed with
Graciously big and thick
It is
My mouth salivates for it
Slurping isn't enough
I want to consume it
Sucking out your energy
Tastes better than treats
I am ready for the travel
Freeing myself all over your penis
To space I cum and I go
On this rollercoaster ride
I am giving you
This duty gives me pleasure!
Birthday sex!

Lust, Pain & Love

LUST

Filled with lust
My mind and body
With sexual desires
His ego inside of my treasure
Day and night
When I awake
Before I go to sleep
Make love to my dreams
Please me when I rise
Toss my salad
Undress it for me
Rough sex but sensual
Seize the moments
Yearning for your soul
Waterfalls my vagina has become
Thinking of you
All you have done
For me
To my body
I love when we become one
Climaxed
In Lust

Lust, Pain & Love

LUSTING

You have me so Gone
Out of body experience
Gone in Ecstasy
Rekindling the thoughts of your ego
Daydreaming
Creaming
Lusting to freak you
Finger in my hidden hole
While I ride you
Forever in lust with you
Your body
I love when our tongues tangle
Touching and serenading my body
Chemistry
No soul connection
Just Soul ties
Through Lust

Lust, Pain & Love

FEELING

Addicted
Aroused
Stimulated
Thrilled
Enticed
Excited
Whet
Sexy
Exotic
Horny
Feminine
Dickmitized
Sprung
Lustful
Happy
Hopeless
Helpless
Sad
Feening your Love!

Lust, Pain & Love

INSIDE OF ME

I feel the intensity of your manhood
As it grows inside of me
Rocking hard as it brushes up against my soul
Feeding my appetite
As you enter and exit
This feeling I am feeling is Bewitching
You have taken over my soul
With your enormous expression
I need it in my throat now!
To taste the blessing that you have been given
I want you to shower all over me
Your seeds of expression
Give until I can take no more
I must consume all of you
As I lightly stroke your jewels with my palms
I love it when your manhood enters my openings;
I wish we could be one for eternity
I need you inside of me to complete me
Help me set aside all my fears
Inside of Me!

Lust, Pain & Love

PLEASE TOUCH MY SOUL

I need you now
I need you more
Please touch my soul
Before you go
Penetrate my mind
While I have you inside
Please touch my soul
I'm wide open
Now enter inside
The gates of heaven
You will feel
As you touch my soul.

Lust, Pain & Love

PART II

PAIN

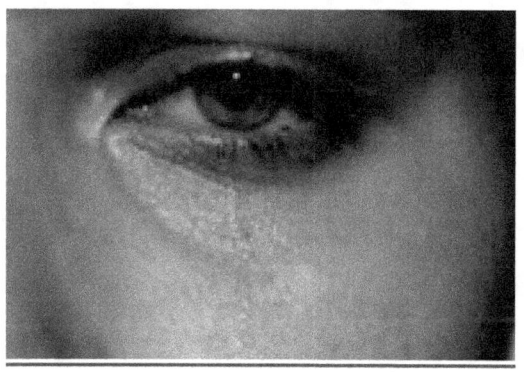

Lust, Pain & Love

WHY NOT STAY?

It is
So easy for you to Leave
Me Alone
In this Broken Home
Where I am weak without you
Facing dehydration without your lips
Where I cant sleep without you near
My Mind I am loosing
These tears they keep on falling
Down my face
As I try to erase this pain that I feel
I cannot think without you
Why not Stay
And Caress my Body with your Tongue
Why not Stay
And embrace me with your Brain
Why do you Run away
So easy is it for you to run away from me
Why Not Stay
Receive this passion that runs Soul deep
Why Not Stay
And Cuddle your tongue against mine
I just want you to Hold my Body Tight
And Make me feel Safe
Why not Stay
When I'm protecting you with my Wings!

LIKE YOU

When I tell you I Love you
Are you disposing me
Putting me in the same category
As the ones before me
Your guard is up
I know your guard is up
But why with me
Have I not showed you Loyalty?
I ask for your hand in Love
But you abandon me
Your emotion less and it shows
Yet my soul won't let you go
My Love For you Runs Deep
Deeper than what you see
Deeper than what you know
See no one has ever captivated me
Like You
No one has ever Sexed me
Like You
No one has ever Listened to me
Like You
Yet you keep Rejecting me
When I am here Only for You
When no one else can Steal your Crown
You are a GOD in my Eyes
A Prophet in Disguise
My King
I'm All Eyes & Ears
My Heart Is Unconditional for you!

DELUSIONAL

Is this real what I feel
Is this real what I see
Or is my mind
Taking over
With these thoughts
That I believe
To be True
Delusions it may be
Delusional I maybe
You are mine
In my mind
No one else can prescribe
Me for this diagnosis
Of what you are
To me
Believe me
You will See
My Husband
Your Wife
I am in Disguise
Your Queen
Undying is my Love
Senile I will be
For the rest of my delusional eternity!

Lust, Pain & Love

SICKENING

My stomach is in pain
In knots
So sick I feel
Within my stomach
Betrayal contest you won
First Prize Winner
No runner up
Sickening to my soul
For you have hurt me so
Before my eyes
Too blind to see
Recognize the signs
Red flags
That were in sight
Disgusted within
Urgent help I need
Of your penis inside of me
To heal this pain
While our bodies become one
So sickening you are to me!

THE FEAR

This passion I feel for you is undeniable,
unforgettable, unbreakable
But it still feels so deniable, forgettable, and breakable
The fear of you giving up on me
The fear of you turning your back on me
Is killing me
I'm fighting anxiety
I never knew exist
The temptation is creeping at my door
To test if this is it.

ON READ

I know you seen my text
Yet
You didn't reply
Do my feelings mean nothing
Or was it all a Façade
I respond in 2 minutes
I always swallow my pride
Yet
You can go a day
Without responding with your reply
Am I that pathetic
To make you leave me on Read
Or have you moved on?
To the new pussy instead
Is she better than me?
The question I ask myself
To make you resist what we have
And leave me instead.

Lust, Pain & Love

LOST

Lost for words
Can't move or react
Dying slowly inside
How could this be happening?
Matchmade in heaven I perceived
Our souls to have aligned
You inside of me
Cloud Nine
Or was it all a Dream?
I am amazed
That I have found myself
In a maze
Unaligned, unwound
Winding down, spiraling
Out of control

Lust, Pain & Love

WEAK

I am weak to my knees
My knees are shaking
My spine in my back is collapsing
Fever chills are on the arise
I can't bare this pain
Another bullet to the heart
So close to giving up
Weakness has come over me
My mind
My spirit
My soul
My body
Has become weak
Over your lack of presence!

CRYING

Tears falling down my right and left cheek
Uncontrollably
My eyelids are in competition
With each other
Water consumed from pain
Rolling down my neck
Tears won't stop falling
Disappointment felt in my throat
The strain on my face
The strep in my throat
Pain in my stomach
I want this to all erase
As I wipe the tears away!

DREAM

It was you inside of me gripping me close
While you stroked me nice and slow
Ooou I don't want to ever let go
Of you
This has to be a dream
Can't be real
Your penis
Oh its soo soo real
This pleasure is breath taking
Im holding back tears
Stick it in my ass
Hole..
I have no fear..
Cum in my ass
As I break off a tear
Pull it out
Move towards your clit
So soft are your lips
As you French kiss my clit
Oooouuu im cumin
Into another galaxy
You take me there
This has to be a dream
You aren't coming back
For my dream isn't real.

Lust, Pain & Love

LONELINESS

Cuddling under my blanket
Holding my pillows tightly
Wishing and wanting
Hating this feeling
Of loneliness
I don't want to feel alone
Yet I feel so alone
Especially when you are gone
Loneliness has struck
With a switch from the tree branch
I must contain
I must not maintain
This feeling
That I have in my heart
My soul, my entire being
Must be released
From you

THE PAIN

Emotionally drained
My Spirit is Weaken
This physical pain
Has me Weeping
Lost without words
I am enduring
Without you beside me
So close to my heart
As you were inside of me
Lust from the start
True Love within my Heart
Its hard to tell
When my Heart is in Hell

Lust, Pain & Love

DYING

End it all
Is what my emotions is telling me
Not worthy of love
Is what my mind is telling me
He's not coming back
Is what my heart is telling me
Anxiety attack
Is what my body is telling me
Loosing control
Is what my mind is telling me
I can no longer breathe
Is what my soul is telling me
Its no longer worth the fight
Is what my spirit is showing me
I no longer want to be
If its not your soul next to me
Dying inside
Since you Escaped from me

Lust, Pain & Love

ABANDONED

Washed hands over me
Discarded
No response
Pulled out
Left on read
Forsaken
The thoughts of what we shared
How inseparable it felt
Cast away it has become
Chickened out so
Reality is not faced
Abandoned he left me
Back to the dust on the ground
I have found
Myself
Abandoned

NEVER AGAIN

No repetition
It won't happen
Again
To me
Pardon you
Please
Come correct
To me
Value is noted
Respect will be given
No more pain
To be felt
Never again
Will I pretend
To ignore what is seen
From within
My third eye

BITTER

Anger
Frustration
Hurt
Resentment
Daily bread
When prospects Approach me
Not interested
Do not speak to me
Heart broken
Trust Issues
Bitterness
Unsweetened
Acid
Tart
Let me Be
Stuck in my Bitterness
It's my Misery

Lust, Pain & Love

Lust, Pain & Love

PART III

LOVE

Lust, Pain & Love

___WITHIN___

Intune within
Focused on Me
Gaining myself
Never settling
Self-worth is Won
Priceless it has become
Trusting the God Within
Me, myself, and I
Internal abundance
Overflow with gratitude
My cup runneth over
With favor
With love
Within

Lust, Pain & Love

DESERVE

Finished holding back
Done fighting this emotion
I deserve you
I deserve this
You love me
Your actions show
Its proven to me
Let us make memories
That will last
For all a legacy
Half on a baby
You not getting rid of me
We deserve this
True love with true intent!

Lust, Pain & Love

ALIGNING

This aligning feels so right
Who would of thought?
Who would of knew?
Perfect timing
A Universal aligning
With reasoning
To be together
Pure intentions
No objectives
With clear conscious
For Eternity
Let's Fulfill our passions
Walk into our purpose
Together
Through this Aligning
The Universe has Won!

NOT GUARDED

My guard was up
Until you broke it
Weak to my knees
Is how you got me
I am so in love
I cannot sleep
Daydreaming about you
I'd rather do
You mean so much to me
Please don't ever Leave!

Lust, Pain & Love

HAND SELECTED

Hand selected
From the Universe
Just for me
Molded in the areas
Of my desires
In areas that fell short
To serve me properly
God knew
When I could not see
I almost gave up
On love
You reconnected my soul
This is spiritual
No one can ever replace
How can they compare
Real Man
You are to me
Hand picked
First Class Selection
Hand-picked for me!

Lust, Pain & Love

ATTACHED

So attached
I am
I love when you are next to me
Hugging you tightly
Our lips reuniting
On a daily
An amazing ceremony
I can renew my soul with yours
Every day for eternity
Walk into destiny
Hand-in-hand
Heart-to-heart
Flow like the waves of the ocean
Mind on cloud nine
A perfect ten
We are
Connected until the end
I am so attached
To you!

Lust, Pain & Love

YOU ARE

Mind fucking me slow
You are
Heavy on my mind
As I feel my vagina moistening
So sexy, so fine and sweet
You are
I just want to retreat
With you on the beach
In the heat
Tongue down your throat
Mouthfucking me slow
Hold on tight
I won't let go
This time
Around,
I got you heavy on Repeat
There's no rotation
You are
Unique
Grand Prize, You Won Me
So Incredible
You Are
No one can Compete
Hands down
You Are!

Lust, Pain & Love

AMUSED

I'm amused
When I think of you
Pulse pounding fast
When I'm next to you
A reconnection felt so strong
Physical aligned with spiritual
My thoughts you have possessed
For I have desired u
For so long
Gracious you are
With your tongue
I'm Cuming fast
To your drum
Off beat my body has become
Your touch has me over the clouds
This is mind blowing
Don't disappear
Away from the shadows of me
Reawaken your soul to the possibilities
Of forever.

Lust, Pain & Love

LOVE FOR YOU

Words can't describe
This feeling my soul yearns for you
It's passionate
Running Deep
Like the River in a Valley Creek
Powerful
Yet So intense
Profound my Heart
When I seek Within
The Love I have for you
Is Extraordinary
I'm Still
In disbelief
This feeling is so surreal
Unreal
Pinch myself to Believe
This is not a Fairytale
I Love you so much
Can't you tell?

PASSION

My passion for you
Runs through my veins
So deeply rooted
It's not for the eyes
The surface
Or spiritually weak
Soul connection
Beyond the lust of human flesh
I feel it in my spine
So passionate in truth
Concrete, I'm passionately in love with you!

Lust, Pain & Love

MATCH MADE

Match made in heaven
Is what my mind is telling me
Match made in heaven
Is what my body is telling me
Match made in heaven
Is what I want to believe
You seem so perfect to me
Could this all be a dream
Or even a gimmick
You are all I want
You are all I need
Match made in heaven
Is what I want you to be.

SOUL SEX

Insertion of your penis
Feels magical
Our souls reuniting as one
Singing a love song
Fine tuning and seizing the memories
Long stroke me slow
As we make music sounds
From our bodies
Moaning to the chorus
Sounds so well
Lift me up in the air
As you stroke me up and down
Lick me as you grip tight my hair
Put me back down to the ground
Flip me over
Take as much air out of me
Without killing
My Soul

BOUND

Bound to your body
My spirit and soul
You connect
This is rare
I can't escape
Whipped I am
From your Smoothness
Authentic and Natural
Demeanor on life
Bound to never leaving
Your side
Sitting passenger side
Sprung is an understatement
I long for this prize
Bound in a ceremonial
Of love
With two souls
Bound

Lust, Pain & Love

IN LOVE

My love for you
Is beyond this realm
I'm beyond the firmament with emotions
Heartfelt for you
I cherish you beyond words
Delightful within your presence
Devoted to you
In passion and truth
Enslaved to never leaving your side
Oh, how I am so in love with you!

I LOVE YOU

Patient and kind
So genuine
Spiritually divine
Nonjudgmental
Flaws and all
Accept me for me
Love me for free
No title
Just let it be
A true love
That was Manifested
Just for Me
I Love You
Forever and Eternity!

UNCONDITIONAL

Trials we won
Together
Hand N Hand
Victory was Ours
We made it
Through the Storms
The Assessments
We passed
Our Love is So Strong
Together
We graduated from Lust
Its Official
Certified in Trust
Unconditional Love
Came from Above
Sent down from Heaven
One
We are
Within Each other
Accepted Flaws
Short comings Granted
While you keep me Cumming
Off your Big Ego
Your tongue
Its Immaculate
I Love you Forever
Unconditional Lover
Lifetime of Happiness
Greatness within you
My love for you is Solid

Lust, Pain & Love

MORE BOOKS & JOURNALS FROM AUTHOR DEE EVANS

"Thoughts From A Black Woman"

"Devotion, Inspiration & God's Word"

"God's Voice for Prayers: 45 Psalms & Prayers"

"30-Day Devotional & Inspiration for the Single Mom"

"Rise Up in Faith: Forgiveness & Repentance"

"Lust, Pain & Love: A Poetry Collection"

"Her Price is far above Rubies: 90-day Self-Reflection Journal"

"Black Girls in Faith: A Righteous Guide for Women"

"She Can, She Will: A 365 Undated Manifestation Daily To-Do Life Planner"

"Daily Planner for Working Moms"

ABOUT DEE EVANS

Dee Evans is a servant of the Most High, Wife, and Mother. She is on a mission to write books to inspire, motivate, and uplift your spirit.
Dee is also the Founder and CEO of Rise2Write Publishing LLC, Poet, 2xPodcaster, and Life Coach.

Check out Dee's Podcasts Streaming on Youtube & all major streaming sites:
"Dee Poetry & Inspiration Podcast" and "Black Girls in Faith Podcast"

If interested in sharing your story with the world through publishing, please visit:
www.rise2write.com

www.ingramcontent.com/pod-product-compliance
Lightning Source LLC
Chambersburg PA
CBHW071906070526
44583CB00016B/1861